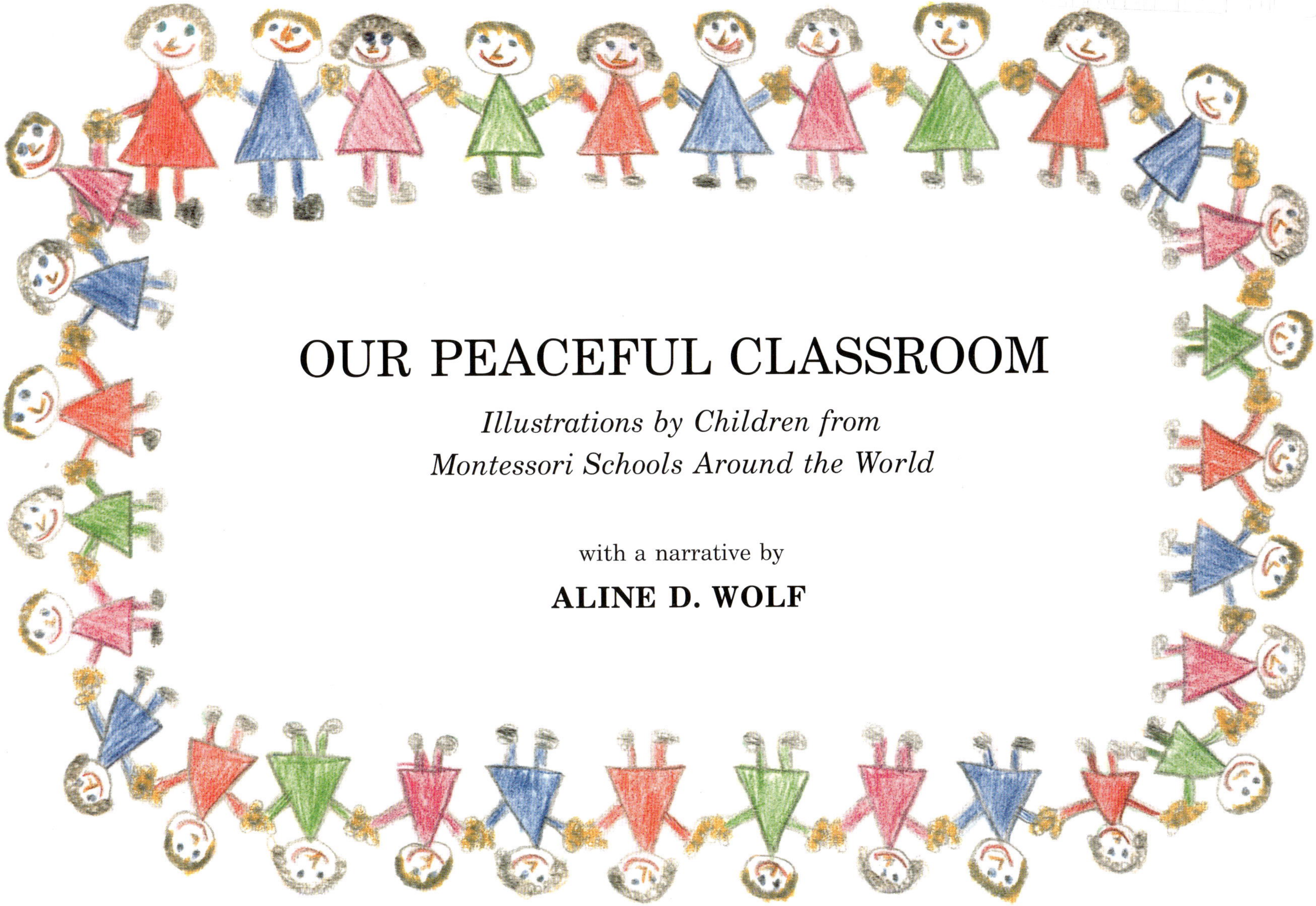

OUR PEACEFUL CLASSROOM

*Illustrations by Children from
Montessori Schools Around the World*

with a narrative by

ALINE D. WOLF

PARENT CHILD PRESS
A division of Montessori Services
www.montessoriservices.com

*Dedicated with love
to all the parents and teachers
who have made
Penn-Mont Academy possible
and to the children
who have always made
this Montessori school so joyful*

Copyright © 1991 Aline D. Wolf
All rights reserved. No part of this book may be used
or reproduced in any manner whatsoever without written
permission except in the case of brief quotations
embedded in critical articles and reviews.

ISBN # 978-0-939195-04-6 (Paperback Edition)
ISBN # 978-0-939195-54-1 (Hardcover Edition)
Library of Congress Control Number: 2017906652

Printed in Korea
Reprint 2018

A division of Montessori Services
www.montessoriservices.com

We go to a Montessori school.

Our classroom is a very happy place.

It is bright and cheerful.

We keep everything neatly on our shelves.

Every day we choose the material we want to work with.

If we don't know how to use it, our teacher helps us.

When we finish our work, we put the material back in its place.

Sometimes two of us want to use the same material at the same time. We might start to fight over it.

Then our teacher tells us that hands are for helping, not for hurting.

Our teacher asks us to think of a better way to decide who can use it.

We decide to take turns because that is the most peaceful way.

We learn to care for everything at our school.
We all help to keep it clean.
We try to carry everything carefully.
If we spill anything, we sweep it up.

I'm Painting

We are learning to make pretty things.

And our classroom is beautiful with fresh flowers and lovely paintings.

Peace is Love and Caring.

We try to speak nicely to each other and to be kind.

We are also learning to help other people
and to make friends with anyone who is all alone.

Sometimes we play the silence game.
When we play this game, everyone holds very still and stops talking.
Then we can listen to our thoughts.

It is very quiet and peaceful.

We are learning to care about nature.

We water our plants.

We feed our fish.

We take care of our animals.

And we try not to hurt any plants or animals anywhere.

We are also learning all about the Universe.

Our planet is "Earth."
It is very old.

We want to take care of our Earth because it gives us what we need for living.

Our Earth gives us air to breathe, water to drink and soil to grow our food.
We want to keep our Earth clean.

When we go for a walk, we pick up papers that other people threw on the ground.

We sort our trash for recycling.

And we never throw any trash in our lakes or rivers or oceans.

Water is very precious. It gives us fish for food.

After we use water in our classroom,
we turn it off carefully so we don't waste it.

Sometimes we ask why our school is called a Montessori school.

Our teacher tells us that Montessori is the last name of a woman who loved children. Her first name was Maria, and she was born in Italy in 1870.

Maria Montessori wanted to help children everywhere to love learning.

So she made beautiful materials for Montessori classrooms.

The materials in our classroom are like the ones that Maria Montessori made.

When Maria Montessori was living, she travelled to many different countries around the world.

She wanted children everywhere to learn about each other.

In our classroom we are studying about many different countries. We have a puzzle map of every continent, and we have flags of many countries.

On video we see pictures of children who live in faraway places.
And we read books about them.

If any of us have pretty things from foreign countries, we bring them to class to show everyone.

49

We had a cuckoo clock from Germany.

We had chopsticks from China.

And a doll

with three other dolls inside her

from Russia (formerly a part of the Soviet Union).

Sometimes we have visitors from foreign countries.

Our visitor from Mexico wore a sombrero.

Our visitor from India wore a sari.

And our visitor from Nigeria played bongo drums.

We like to learn about people from other countries.

And we also learn about the great peacemakers.

They teach us to make friends with everyone.

We hope to grow up in a peaceful world.

AFTERWORD

Maria Montessori's philosophy of education has always seemed to me to be a blueprint for peace. For the classroom environment she prescribed order, serenity, and beauty. Her precepts for behavior of both teachers and children rest on the ideal of respect for others and for the property of others. Learning is cooperative, not competitive, and everyday conflicts are resolved with a sense of fairness. In the Silence Game, even three-year-olds are made aware of their own inner quiet. And no child is too young to learn to appreciate the value of other cultures, beginning with beautiful geography materials.

This atmosphere of peace is often taken for granted by Montessori students. In other words, it is implicit in their environment, but it is not usually explicit in their consciousness—their thoughts, their conversations, or their artwork. It may be only years later, when they are in more chaotic situations, that they look back and recognize the peacefulness of their early years in Montessori.

Recently I have come to believe that we, as adults, can help Montessori children raise this precious early experience from an unconscious to a conscious level, by pointing out the peaceful elements in their classroom, inviting them to verbalize their feelings on the subject, and to express these feelings in their artwork. The book you are holding is the result of this process carried out in a variety of Montessori classrooms throughout the world.

Children between the ages of four and twelve provided all the illustrations in this volume. All these children were either in a Montessori class for three- to six-year-olds or they had been in such a class in previous years.

We at Parent Child Press were overwhelmed by the generous response to our announcement of plans for this book. Hundreds of pieces of artwork arrived from both near and distant locations. The quality of many of the paintings was so outstanding that it was difficult for us to make the necessary eliminations. In doing so, we ultimately had to choose for publication those that best illustrated the message of the narrative and fit comfortably into the artistic design of the book.

My thanks to all the children who provided artwork for the project and to their teachers who talked with them about peace, encouraged their participation, screened the submissions, and carefully packaged and mailed the selections from their schools.

I stand in awe of the insights, the creativity, and the ability of all the children who participated in this project.

Aline D. Wolf
Fort Meyers, FL
January 2018

The Illustrators

Ivonne Nuñez Ponce Age 12
Taller Infantil De Artes Plasticas
Cd. Juarez, Chihuahua, MEXICO
Cover

Suzanne Marie Kobb Age 10
Little Flower Montessori Elementary
Mishawaka, IN
Title Page

Cathie Korinek Age 5
Fox Valley Montessori School
Aurora, IL
Page 2

Ashley Williams Age 4
Montessori Academy
Mobile, AL
Page 3

Latoya Brownlee Age 8
Fox Valley Montessori School
Aurora, IL
Page 4

Shelly Prather Age 8
Treetops School
Euless, TX
Page 5

Joy Moy Age 6
White Bear Montessori School
White Bear Lake, MN
Page 6

Evans Sanders Beach Age 9
Center for Education
Bradenton, FL
Page 7

Blair Waugh Age 7
Amelia Island Montessori School
Amelia Island, FL
Page 8

Ellen Riley Age 6
Penn-Mont Academy
Altoona, PA
Page 9

Anya Buckhard Age 7
Treetops School
Euless, TX
Page 10

Etienne Bertie Age 8
Blaisdale Montessori School
Scarborough, Ontario, CANADA
Page 11

Jeremy Shlachter Age 7
E.M. Daggett Elementary
Ft. Worth, TX
Page 12

Sam Naney Age 5
Little Star Montessori School
Winthrop, WA
Page 13

Alicia Au Age 9
New Horizons Montessori School
Ft. Washington, PA
Page 14

Rachel Hollander Age 5
Penn-Mont Academy
Altoona, PA
Page 15

Marisa Vitto Age 7
Gulf Stream School
Gulf Stream, FL
Page 16

Bianca TriBazio Age 6
Amelia Island Montessori School
Amelia Island, FL
Page 17

Julia Zdrahal Age 6
Wa Ora Montessori School
Naenai, Wellington, NEW ZEALAND
Page 18

Samantha Zdrahal Age 8
Wa Ora Montessori School
Naenai, Wellington, NEW ZEALAND
Page 19

Katie Sovinski Age 11
Little Flower Montessori Elementary
Mishawaka, IN
Page 20

Katie Bradley Age 11
Little Flower Montessori Elementary
Mishawaka, IN
Page 21

James Joseph Riley Age 6
Calumet Region Montessori School
Hobart, IN
Page 22

Marti Garrett Age 6
Village Montessori Schools
Carmichael, CA
Page 23

Rebecca Asta Age 8
Plenty Valley Montessori School
Diamond Creek, Victoria, AUSTRALIA
Page 24

Whitney Tiernan Age 7
Gulf Stream School
Gulf Stream, FL
Page 25

Matthew Tyler Age 5
Stillwater Montessori School
Old Town, ME
Page 26

Stephen Nightingale Age 10
Dearcroft Montessori School
Oakville, Ontario, CANADA
Page 27

Ryan Rieber Age 6
E.M. Daggett Elementary
Ft. Worth, TX
Page 28

Laura Byington Age 5
Rising Star School
Alameda, CA
Page 29

Justin Burkhart Age 8
Center for Education
Bradenton, FL
Page 30

Logann Gavey Age 7
Rising Star School
Alameda, CA
Page 31

Javier Del Vasto Sánchez Age 11
Escuela Montessori de Panamá
Panamá, REPUBLIC OF PANAMÁ
Page 32

Javier Jesús Paredes Reyes Age 10
Escuela Montessori de Panamá
Panamá, REPUBLIC OF PANAMÁ
Page 33

Veronica Mancilla Beutelspacher Age 8
Taller Infantil De Artes Plasticas
Cd. Juarez, Chihuahua, MEXICO
Page 34

Ryan Rieber Age 6
E.M. Daggett Elementary
Ft. Worth, TX
Page 35

Miguel Angel Seanez Madrid Age 9
Taller Infantil De Artes Plasticas
Cd. Juarez, Chihuahua, MEXICO
Page 36

Dale R. Balsis Age 5
Nazareth Montessori School
Pago Pago, AMERICAN SAMOA
Page 37

Saarene Panossian Age 11
New Horizons Montessori School
Ft. Washington, PA
Page 38

Rachel Joseph Age 6
Penn-Mont Academy
Altoona, PA
Page 39

Lydia Peeples Age 7
Amelia Island Montessori School
Amelia Island, FL
Page 40

Katy Gore Age 9
Center for Education
Bradenton, FL
Page 41

Sarah Nankervis Age 7
Plenty Valley Montessori School
Diamond Creek, Victoria, AUSTRALIA
Page 42

Greg Waltz Age 11
New Horizons Montessori School
Ft. Washington, PA
Page 43

Julia Funk   Age 8
New Horizons Montessori School
Ft. Washington, PA
Page 44

Cassandra D. Chelf   Age 6
Calumet Region Montessori School
Hobart, IN
Page 45

David Emlyn Fanner   Age 5
Brooksfield School
McLean, VA
Page 46

Barton Jordan   Age 11
Gulf Stream School
Gulf Stream, FL
Page 47

Laura Amar-Dolan   Age 5
Stillwater Montessori School
Old Town, ME
Page 48

Doug Graham   Age 8
Treetops School
Euless, TX
Page 49

Todd Fleck   Age 10
Treetops School
Euless, TX
Page 50

Clayton Conaway   Age 9
Treetops School
Euless, TX
Page 51

Katie Maresca   Age 11
Christian Family Montessori School
Mt. Ranier, MD
Page 52

Aaron Gilbert   Age 11
Penn-Mont Academy
Altoona, PA
Page 53

Ellen Riley   Age 6
Penn-Mont Academy
Altoona, PA
Page 54

Sandra Gaughan   Age 10
New Horizons Montessori School
Ft. Washington, PA
Page 55

Amy McCann   Age 12
Fox Valley Montessori School
Aurora, IL
Page 56

Emilie Bulette   Age 11
New Horizons Montessori School
Ft. Washington, PA
Page 57

Tierre Fields   Age 6
Gloria Dei Montessori
Dayton, OH
Page 58

Sarita Lynn Simon   Age 6
Gloria Dei Montessori
Dayton, OH
Page 59

Ezra Waddell   Age 11
High Park Montessori School
Toronto, Ontario, CANADA
Page 60

Katie Riley   Age 4
Penn-Mont Academy
Altoona, PA
Page 63

Blair Waugh   Age 7
Amelia Island Montessori School
Amelia Island, FL
Page 64

Deborah Kobb   Age 11
Little Flower Montessori Elementary
Mishawaka, IN
Back Cover

The age given for each child is the age when the illustration was made.

The Montessori school listed for each child is either the school presently attended or the school attended in earlier years.

About the Author

Aline Wolf, through her writing and lecturing, is widely regarded as a modern interpreter of Maria Montessori. Mrs. Wolf has authored 27 books for teachers, parents, or children, all based on Montessori principles, including the classics *A Parents' Guide to the Montessori Classroom* and *Nurturing the Spirit in Non-Sectarian Classrooms*. Her latest book, *Montessori For a Better World*, is a compilation of her most significant writings with new chapters focusing on the purpose of education for the common good.

Recognizing that Montessori techniques were a delightful means of introducing beautiful paintings to young children, Mrs. Wolf wrote a manual, *How to Use Child-Size Masterpieces for Art Appreciation* (formerly *Mommy, It's a Renoir!*), describing hands-on art appreciation activities. She then created a series of eight companion books—*Child-Size Masterpieces*—featuring reproductions appropriate for these activities.

In 1989 Mrs. Wolf highlighted Montessori's overall commitment to peace in a book that challenged both parents and teachers—*Peaceful Children, Peaceful World* (now out-of-print). As a sequel to this, *Our Peaceful Classroom* challenges the children to peaceful existence in our global community.

About the Designer

Jana Stanford Sidler has designed a variety of logos and publications throughout her career in the advertising field in Buffalo, New York and Altoona, Pennsylvania. Many of her designs have received awards which have credited her success as a commercial designer. She began her freelance career while teaching design at Buffalo State College.

Presently teaching art at Bishop Guilfoyle High School in Altoona, she devotes her time between broadening the awareness of the arts in children and producing various publications in her design studio. This is the third book on which she has collaborated with Aline Wolf.

About Maria Montessori

Maria Montessori (1870-1952) was born in Italy and became known throughout the world as a great educational innovator. Trained in science and medicine, she used her skillful powers of observation to analyze young children's most natural and effective learning strategies that she found rooted in a series of sensitive periods. To enhance these early learning periods, she then designed an ingenious series of hands-on educational materials, reproductions of which are still used in Montessori classrooms on every continent.

More important than her materials, however, is Maria Montessori's philosophy that enables both teachers and parents to have a very comfortable and fruitful relationship with youngsters. Basic to all her efforts for reform is her conviction that civilization can be saved by children who are respected as individuals, nourished by caring adults, and educated for peace.